Gifted & Talented®

BRAIN Games

For Ages 6-8

By Vicky Shiotsu
Illustrated by Sean Parkes

Lowell House Juvenile

NTC Publishing Group

Viva Books Private Limited

First South Asian Edition 2000

VIVA BOOKS PRIVATE LIMITED

- 4262/3 Ansari Road, Daryaganj, New Delhi 110 002
  E-mail: viva@vivagroupindia.net
- 215-216 New Apollo Estate, 2nd Floor, Mogra Lane, Andheri (E), Mumbai 400 069 E-mail: vivamumbai@vivagroupindia.net
- Jamals Fazal Chambers, 26 Greams Road, Chennai 600 006
  E-mail: vivachennai@vivagroupindia.net
- B-103, Jindal Towers, 21/1A/3 Darga Road, Kolkata 700 017
  E-mail: vivakolkata@vivagroupindia.net
- 7 GF, Sovereign Park Apts., 56-58 K.R. Road, Basavanagudi, Bangalore 560 004 E-mail: vivabangalore@vivagroupindia.net
- 101 & 102, First Floor, Mughal Marg Apartments, Narayanaguda, Hyderabad 500 029 E-mail: vivahyderabad@vivagroupindia.net

Published by arrangement with

NTC / Contemporary Publishing Group, 4255 West Touhy Avenue, Lincolnwood (Chicago), Illinois 60646-1975, USA

ISBN 81-7649-165-9

Published by Vinod Vasishtha for Viva Books Private Limited
4262/3 Ansari Road, Daryaganj, New Delhi 110 002 and
printed & bound at Raj Press, R-3, Inderpuri, New Delhi 110 012.

NOTE TO PARENTS

Teach a child facts and you give her knowledge. Teach her to think and you give her wisdom. This is the principle behind the entire series of *Gifted & Talented®* materials. And this is the reason that thinking skills are being stressed in classrooms throughout the country.

Gifted & Talented® Brain Games has been designed specifically to promote the development of critical and creative thinking skills. The problems in this exciting book include visual puzzles, logic problems, riddles, science stumpers, sequencing activities, and more! All the problems will spark children's imaginations, sharpen their thinking skills, and foster a love of learning!

The inviting artwork on each page contains clues to some of the answers and provides visual reinforcement for learning. Some of the problems have been grouped so that they give the child practice using a certain type of thinking strategy. For example, two logic problems may be placed side by side so that when the child figures out how to solve the first one, he or she may apply those skills in solving the second one. Each problem, however, can stand alone, and the problems do not have to be done in any particular order.

Your child may be inspired by the problems in this book to create his or her own puzzles! If so, have your child present the problem to you and explain the answer. Praise your child's efforts, and encourage him or her to continue making more puzzles. This type of activity not only stimulates creativity, but it also develops your child's ability to apply different strategies for solving problems.

TIME SPENT TOGETHER

The time you spend with your child as he or she learns is invaluable. This "one-on-one" contact with your child cannot be duplicated at school. The more positive and constructive an environment you can create, the better. Here are some tips to keep in mind as you work with your child:

- Let your child look through the book and choose the problems that interest him or her. The problems in the book are self-contained and do not have to be done sequentially.
- Allow your child to go at his or her own pace. If your child wants to do only one or two pages, accept that and return to the material at another time.
- Give your child time to think about the answers. A common mistake parents and teachers make is to jump in with the answer when a child hesitates. Help your child by rephrasing the question if necessary, or by providing hints or prompts.
- Remember that your child's level of participation will vary at different times. Sometimes a response may be brief and simplistic; at other times, a response may be elaborate and creative. Allow room for both.
- Offer your child praise and encouragement frequently. It is much easier for a child to learn in a secure, accepting environment.

This book will not only teach your child about many things, but it will teach *you* a lot about your child! Make the most of your time together—and have fun!

A SPECIAL WORD

Which word below reads the same whether you hold it right-side up or upside down? Make a guess, and then check your answer.

PUP **NOON** **DID**

MEN **POP** **TOOT**

LOOK IN THE MIRROR

Which words below still read the same when you hold them up to a mirror? Make a guess, and then check your answer.

MOM **EVE**

DAD **OTTO**

SIS **ANNA**

FROM HERE TO THERE

Sheriff Buck rode on horseback from the town of Dustyroads to the town of Goldfever. The trip usually took three days. Sheriff Buck left Dustyroads on Friday and arrived in Goldfever on the same Friday. How did he do that?

HORSING AROUND

Sheriff Buck's horse was tied to a rope that was 8 feet long. The horse saw some hay 20 feet away. The horse was hungry. So, it walked over and ate the hay! Explain how the horse did that.

MAKING MOVES

Can you change two rows of pennies into a circle of pennies? Try it and see! Get six pennies. Put the pennies on a table so that they look like this:

Now change the rows into a circle by moving only two pennies.

GORF'S WORD GAME

Gorf is from a faraway planet. While traveling to Earth, he played a game to pass the time. He wrote the word **planet** on a piece of paper. Gorf erased the letter **e** from the word, and he was left with the word **plant**. Then he erased another letter, and he was left with a word again. Gorf kept erasing the letters one by one. Each time he was left with a word. Even the last letter that was left was a word! In what order did Gorf erase the letters?

SPACE FRIENDS

Look at the letters on the spaceships below. They spell out the word SPACE. How many lines do you need to draw to connect each spaceship to all the other spaceships?

Hint: Write the letters S, P, A, C, and E on a sheet of paper to match the positions in the picture. Then draw lines to find the answer.

GO, TEAM, GO!

The Zops and Snarfs are watching an exciting ball game. Look at the fans. See if you can tell one way that the Zops are alike and one way that the Snarfs are alike.

Now look at the players. Which ones are Zops? Which ones are Snarfs?

CROSSING A RIVER

Mr. Banks and his two sons have to get to the other side of a river in a small boat. The boat can only hold up to 200 pounds. Mr. Banks weighs 160 pounds. Each of his sons weighs 100 pounds. How can they cross the river?

TIME TO BIKE

Minna is planning to ride her bike to Emma's house. Minna is going to take her dog, cat, and mouse to play with. Minna is riding her bike, and she can only take one pet at a time in her bike's basket. She never leaves the cat alone with the dog because it gets chased by the dog if Minna isn't there to protect it! She also never leaves the cat and mouse together because the cat goes after the mouse! How can Minna get her three pets to Emma's house?

COUNT THE TRIANGLES

How many triangles can you find in the shape below?

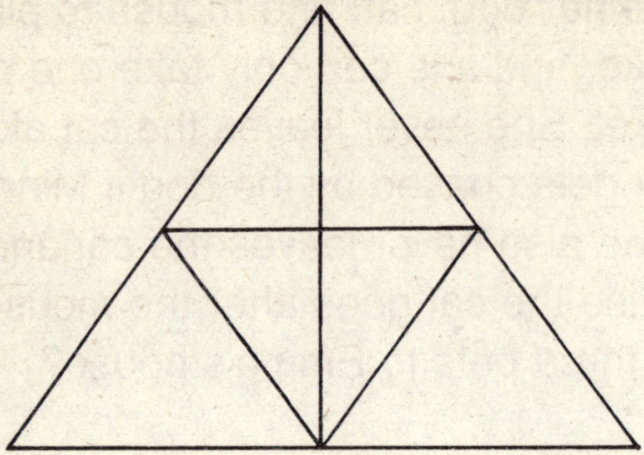

A TRIANGLE CAT

How many triangles can you find in this picture of a cat?

PIECES OF PIE

The baker is going to make three straight cuts across the pie. How can he make the cuts to get seven pieces of pie?

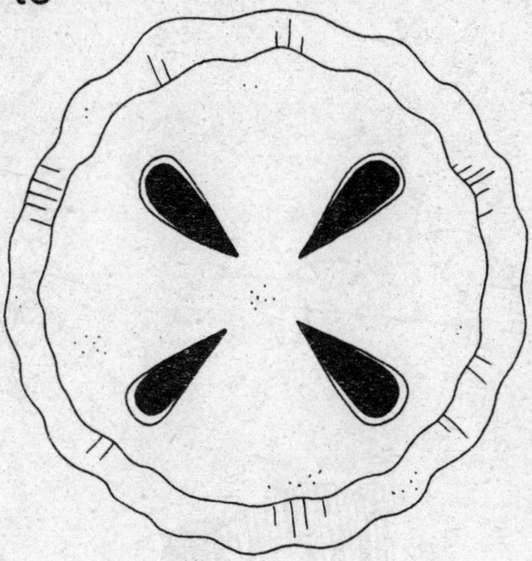

PLAYING WITH FOOD

Bert was eating slices of ham. He took his last slice and cut it into pieces. Then he arranged the pieces on his plate to make a word. What was the word?

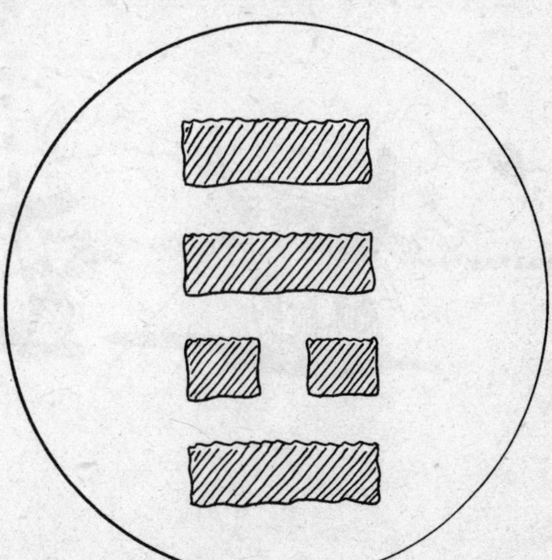

OUT FOR A WALK

The artist who drew this picture made a mistake. What is the mistake?

DOG ON THE RUN

Josh stood on one side of a lake. His dog, Ruff, stood on the other side. "Come on, Ruff!" called Josh. Ruff got excited and started across the lake. He got all the way across without getting wet! How did Ruff do that?

PARROT TALK

Mr. Burns went to a pet shop to buy a bird. When he got there, the sales clerk showed him a parrot. "This parrot is amazing," said the sales clerk. "I guarantee it will repeat every word it hears!"

Mr. Burns bought the parrot. As soon as he got home, he spoke to the bird. But no matter how much Mr. Burns talked, the parrot would not say a single word. Everything the sales clerk said, though, was true. How could that be?

HIDDEN ANIMALS

The name of an animal is hidden in each of the sentences below. The name of the animal in the first sentence has been underlined so that it is easy to see. Find the hidden animal names in the rest of the sentences.

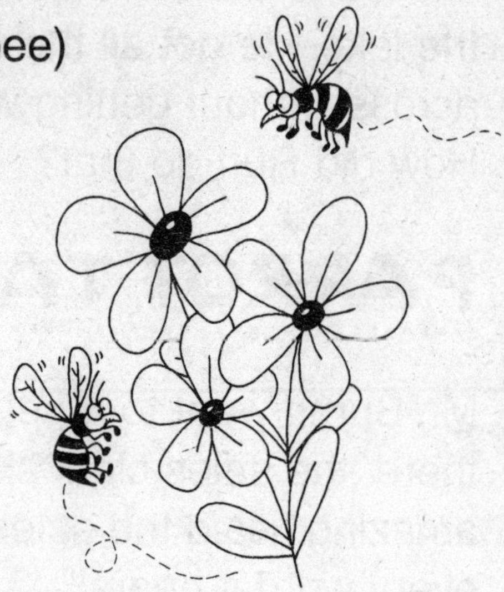

1. Jan will <u>be e</u>leven next week. (bee)
2. We planted some corn.
3. The cake batter is thick.
4. Mandy peeled the apple.
5. We will go at six o'clock.
6. Lee got a bar of soap and a towel.
7. Most rich people have big homes.
8. Ed will keep the watch or sell it.
9. Dad will need to use a ladder.
10. I think Tom will be a very good student.

HIDDEN FOODS

The name of a food is hidden in each of the sentences below. The name of the food in the first sentence has been underlined so that it is easy to see. Find the hidden food names in the rest of the sentences.

1. Bob read a funny story. (bread)

2. There are many kinds of beetles.

3. I put four ice cubes in a glass.

4. Kris will meet me at the park.

5. Tanya wants to be an elephant trainer.

6. Len tied a rope around a tree.

7. Cindy left her pot at our house.

8. We need to wrap plenty of string around the box.

9. We hope a chick will hatch from our egg.

10. My sister likes to pick leaves off the ground.

PENNIES ON A GRID

Draw a large tic-tac-toe grid on a sheet of paper. Get eight pennies and put them on the grid to match the picture below.

There are three pennies along each side of the grid. Move four pennies so that there are four pennies along each side.

ROWS OF PENNIES

Get six pennies. Put them in two lines to match the picture. You will have one line with three pennies and one line with four pennies.

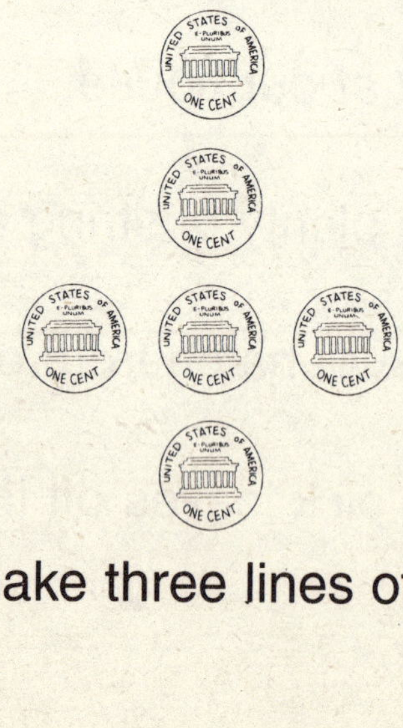

Move one penny to make three lines of three pennies.

A PUZZLING BALL THROW

How can you throw a ball so that it stops, changes direction, and comes back to you?

WHY CAN'T THEY SHAKE HANDS?

Two children are standing on the same sheet of newspaper. They find it impossible to shake hands. How can that be?

MRS. LEE'S LUNCH

Mrs. Lee went to a restaurant for lunch. The signs below tell what she ordered. What did Mrs. Lee have for lunch?

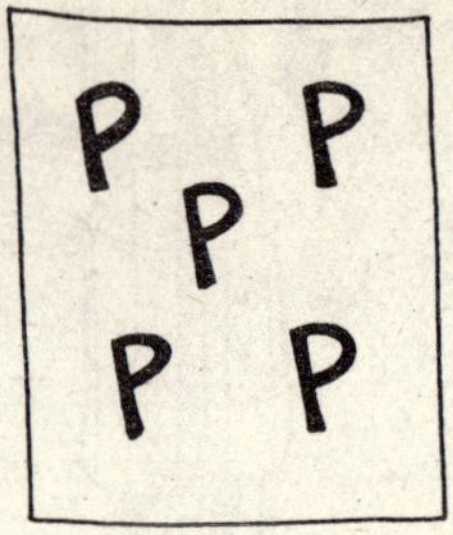

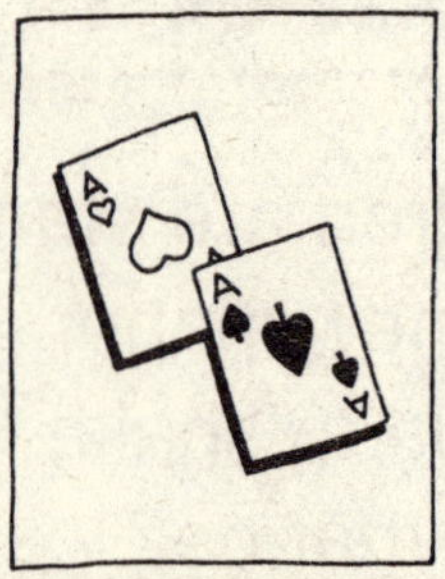

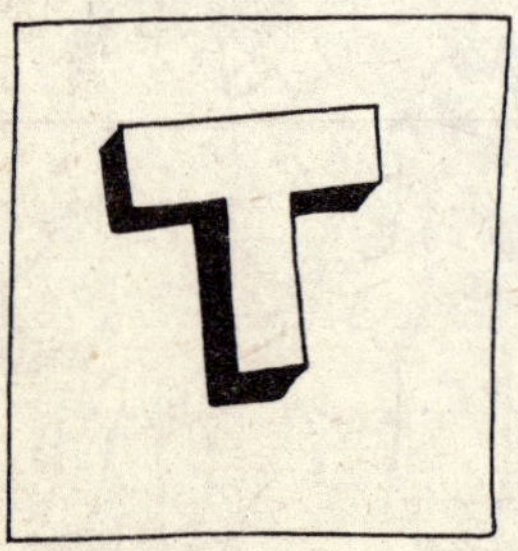

A COLD DRINK

Ricky drew a picture of an ice cube in a glass of water. What mistake did he make?

ON THE ROAD

A woman drove 100 miles in her car without knowing that she had a flat tire. How did that happen?

ACROSS AND DOWN

Suppose you had nine letter cards that spelled these words:

a	p	e

h	a	t

t	e	n

How could you arrange the letters on the grid below so that the words could be read both across and down?
Hint: Copy the grid on a sheet of paper to work out the answer.

ACROSS AND DOWN AGAIN

Suppose you had 16 letter cards that spelled these words:

r	e	s	t

s	t	a	r

t	u	n	e

a	n	t	s

How could you arrange the letters on the grid below so that the words could be read both across and down?
Hint: Copy the grid on a sheet of paper to work out the answer.

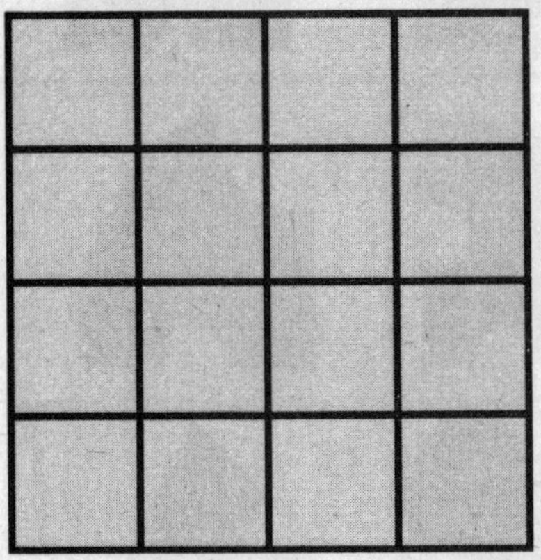

TURN THE SHAPES OVER

Marvin cut out shapes from special paper. The paper is white on one side and black on the other side.

Look at the white shapes labeled 1 to 4. If each white shape was turned over, which black shape would it look like?

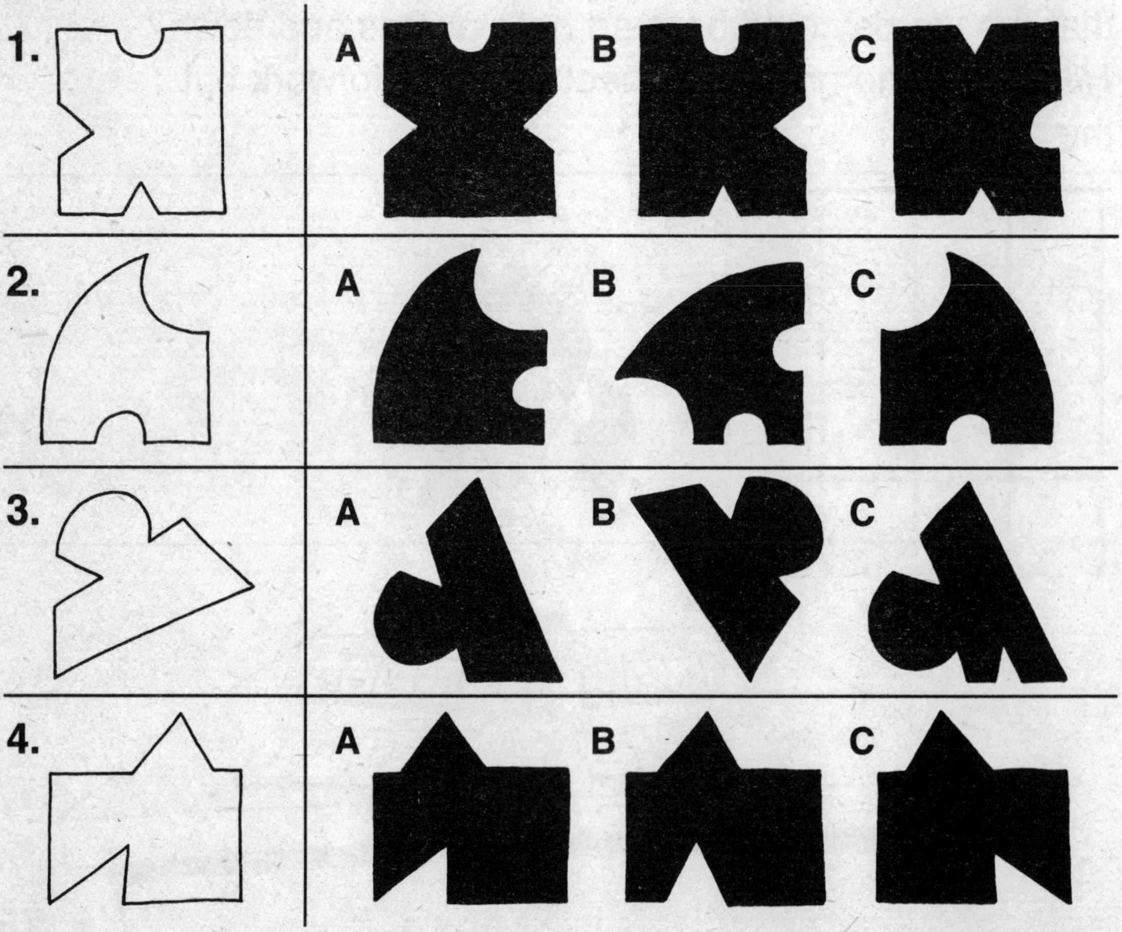

WAITING IN LINE

Mrs. Brown, Miss White, Mrs. Black, and Miss Green are standing in line at the post office. See if you can figure out their order. Read the clues below.

Mrs. Black is between Mrs. Brown and Miss White.

Miss Green is next to Mrs. Brown.

Miss White is not first.

WHAT'S IN THE BOX?

Only one of the children is correct. What is in the box?

SEVEN ELVES

Read this story.

There were three men. They mended fences. The three men met seven wee elves. The elves yelled, "Hey, let's help the men!" The elves were speedy. They mended ten fences. They mended the fences very well. Then the elves helped the men mend fences every week. Whenever the men needed help, the elves were there. The elves were very sweet, weren't they?

There is something unusual about the story. Can you spot what it is?

LOOKING AT LINES

Which line is longer—A, B, or C? Make a guess first. Then check your answer by measuring the lines with a ruler.

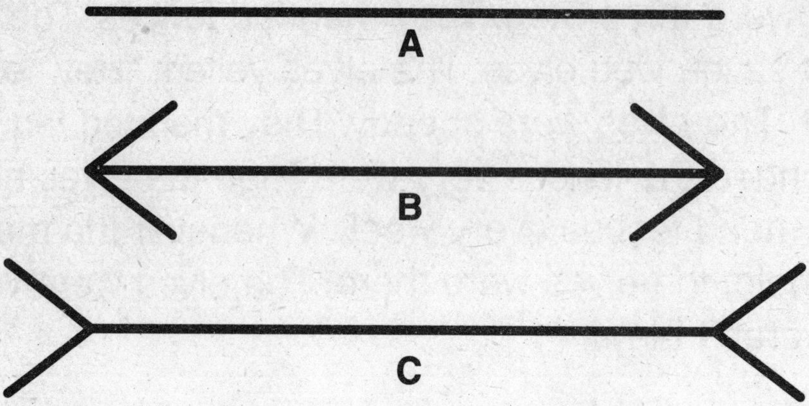

LOOKING AT CIRCLES

Which circle is bigger—A or B? Make a guess first. Then check your answer by measuring across the middle of each circle.

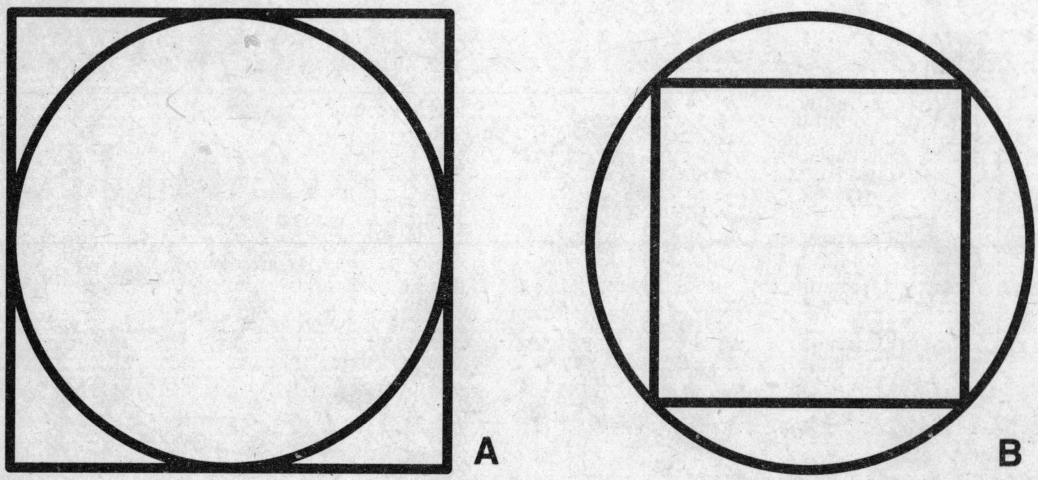

HOW MANY BLOCKS?

Look at the figure below. How many blocks do you see?

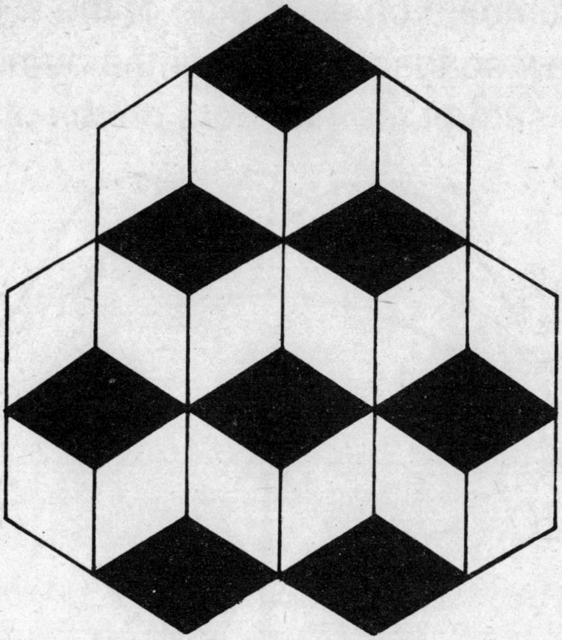

WHAT'S IN THE PIGGY BANK?

There are eight coins in the piggy bank. They add up to 50 cents. What coins are in the bank?

CUTTING TIME IN HALF

Divide the clock in half by placing a straw across it. There should be six numbers on each side of the straw. Now position the straw so that the sum of the numbers on one side equals the sum of the numbers on the other side.

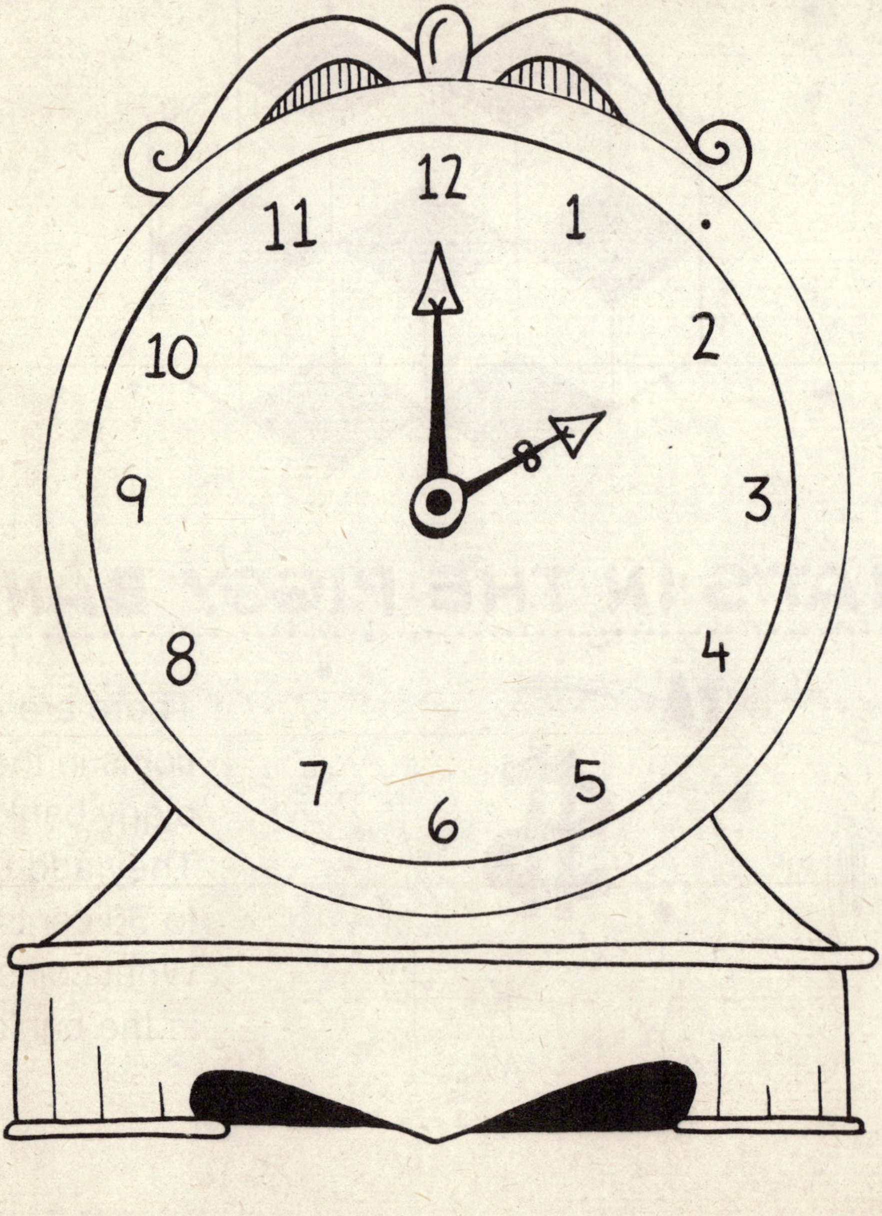

FROM SHORTEST TO TALLEST

The Grant family has five girls. The girls are lined up from shortest to tallest. Read the clues to figure out the name of each girl in the picture.

Patty is taller than Sally.

Betty is taller than Margo.

Margo is taller than Jenny.

Sally is taller than Betty.

THE AMAZING WALDO

Read the following sentence carefully:

The amazing Waldo juggled
forty-six plastic balls very quickly.

What is unusual about the sentence?
Hint: Look very closely at *all* the letters.

DRAW A HOUSE

Draw this house on a sheet of paper using one *continuous* line. This means you can't lift your pencil off the paper once you start, and you can't go over any line twice. Can you do it?

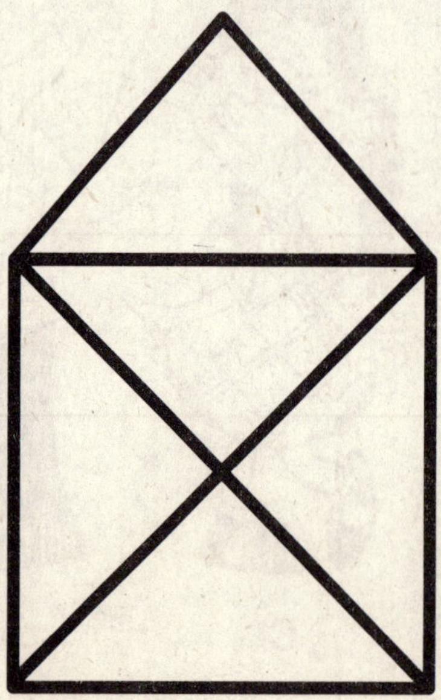

TYING A KNOT

How can you pick up a string with both hands and tie a knot without letting go of either end of the string?

A KNOTTY PROBLEM

If you pull the ends of each rope below, only one will form a knot. Which one?

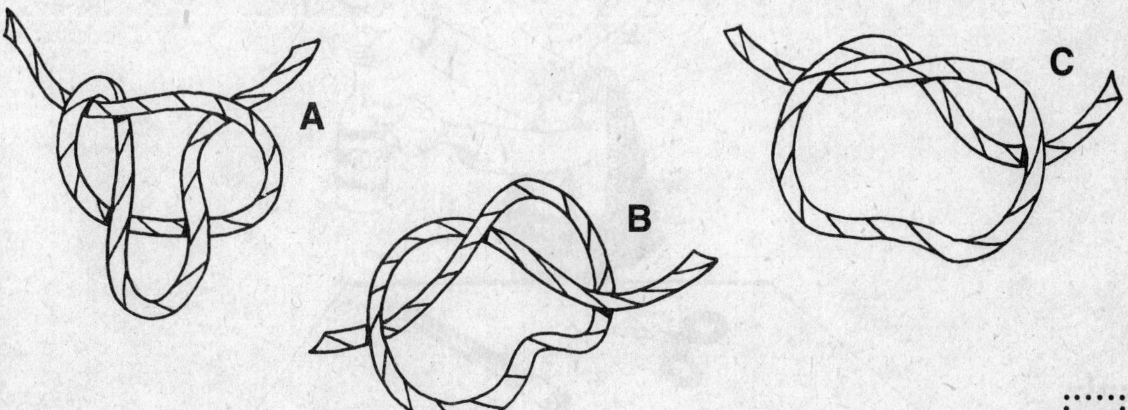

PUSH THE BOTTLE

Here's a fun trick to try!

1. Get paper, scissors, and an empty soda bottle.

2. Cut out a 2-inch paper square.

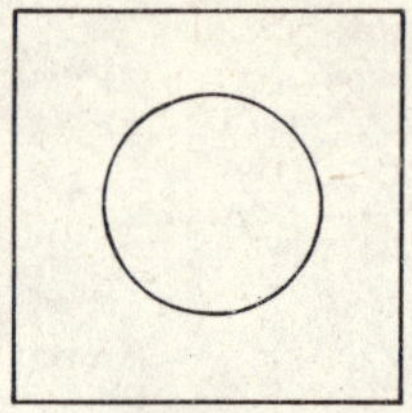

3. Fold the paper in half and cut out a hole that will fit over the neck of the soda bottle.

4. Put the soda bottle on a table. Put the paper square over the neck of the bottle.

5. Without making the hole in the square larger, push the bottle through the hole!

FLIP, FLOP

Get 10 pennies. Lay them out in rows to make a triangle that points up.

Move one penny at a time. In three moves, change the triangle so that it points down.

RISE AND SHINE

Here is a picture of Susie getting ready in the morning. But something is wrong with the picture. Can you spot what it is?

CLAUDIA'S BUG

Look at the spiders and ladybugs. One of them belongs to Claudia. Read the clues to find out which one.
Hint: Columns go up and down. Rows go across.

The bug is in a column that has two spiders.

The bug is in a row that has two ladybugs.

There is no ladybug to the right of the bug.

BO'S APARTMENT

Bo lives in an apartment building. The building is pictured on the next page. Find out which apartment is his. Read the clues below.

There are no plants on my windowsill.

My window has no curtains.

None of the windows above or below my window has plants.

My apartment window is open.

The window above my window has no curtains.

A STRANGE NOTE

Mrs. Jones is always getting unusual notes from her son. Here is a note she got one afternoon. Mrs. Jones found an easy way to figure out what the note said. Can you?

MOM

TUO MA I

.TTAM HTIW

MOT

UPSIDE-DOWN NUMBERS

The number 9 is 6 upside down. The number 6 is 9 upside down. What is 96 upside down? Make a guess, and then check your answer.

ANOTHER STRANGE NOTE

Mrs. Jones got another strange-looking note from her son. She looked at it for a few seconds. Then she smiled. Mrs. Jones found a way to read the note easily. See if you can!

MOM

I DECIDED TO

BIKE WITH MIKE.

I WILL COME

HOME SOON.

TOM.

SENTENCE RIDDLES

Claire made interesting groups of words and pictures. Each group stands for a sentence. See if you can "read" the sentences on this page and the next. The first one has been done for you.

1. 

The dog is under the table.

R
2. We played G THE ROSIE I
N

3. arrest
you're

4. 

5. THE I was lost FOREST

6. Liz bought pants
pants

7. 

8. my bed
my slippers

9. Jack goes to school HOME

PICKY EATERS

Read about the foods these children like and don't like. Then answer the questions.

1. Pam likes apples and oranges, but she doesn't like pineapples or plums. She likes spinach and tomatoes, but she doesn't like potatoes. Does Pam like peas?

2. Scott likes broccoli and beets, but he doesn't like beans or corn. He likes lettuce and carrots, but he doesn't like celery or tomatoes. Does Scott like cabbage?

3. Nicole likes tangerines and blueberries, but she doesn't like apples. She likes potatoes and cucumbers, but she doesn't like cauliflower. Does Nicole like watermelon?

WHAT COMES NEXT?

Look at the figures in each row. Study the pattern. Then, on a separate sheet of paper, draw the figure that should come next.

1. 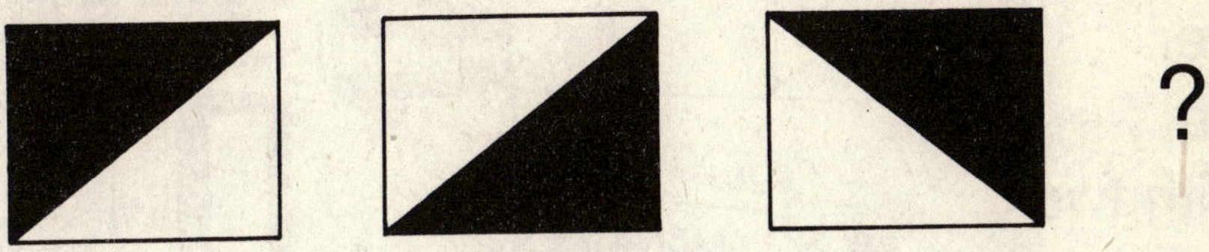

2. 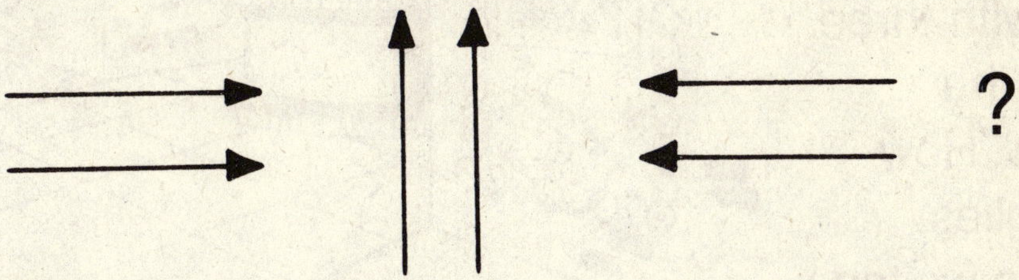

3. 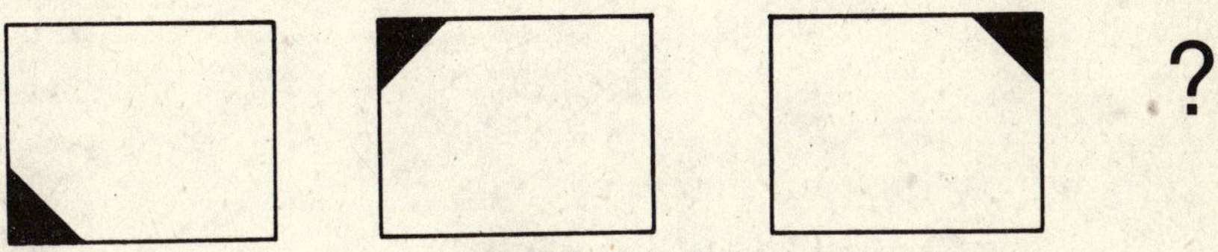

4. 

5. 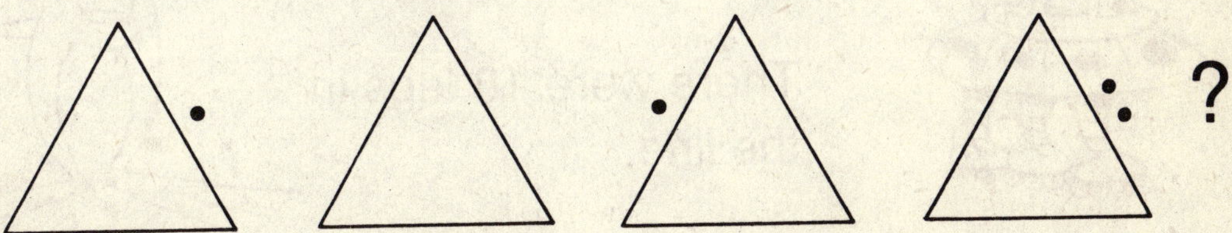

GOOGLIES AND WINKLES

The Space Fantasy Theater invited aliens from all over the galaxy to the opening of a new movie. Some Googlies and Winkles waited in line to get into the movie theater. Googlies are creatures with two legs. Winkles are creatures with three legs. Read the clues below. How many Googlies and Winkles waited in line?

Only Winkles and Googlies waited in line.

There were more Winkles than Googlies.

There were 18 legs in the line.

WHOSE PET?

The Pet-Sitter Clinic was caring for three pets—a dog, a cat, and a rabbit. Mr. Gee, Mr. Dee, and Mrs. Jay came to pick up their pets at four o'clock.

The worker at the clinic looked at the three people and asked, "Which pet belongs to you?"

Mr. Gee said, "I don't own a rabbit."

"Oh, I thought you did," said the man who owned the cat.

Can you figure out which pet belongs to which person?

WHICH LINES MEET?

Look at line A below. If you made it longer, which line would it meet—B or C? Guess first, then place a ruler along line A to check your answer.

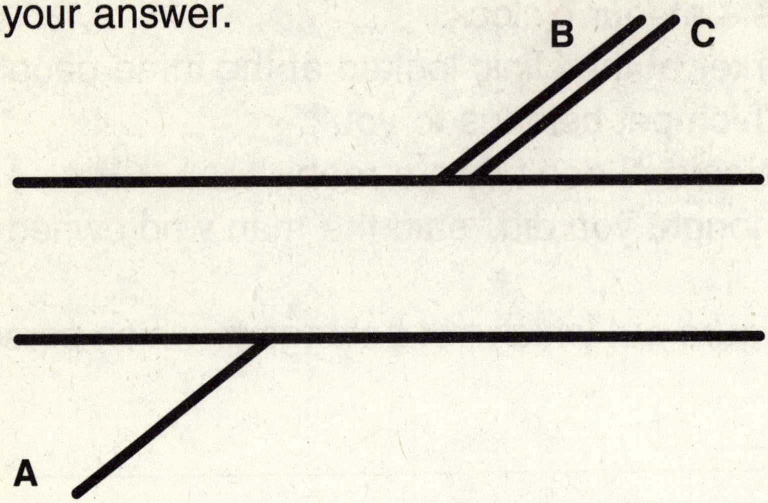

WHICH LINE IS STRAIGHT?

Look at lines A and B. Which line is straight—A, B, neither of them, or both of them?

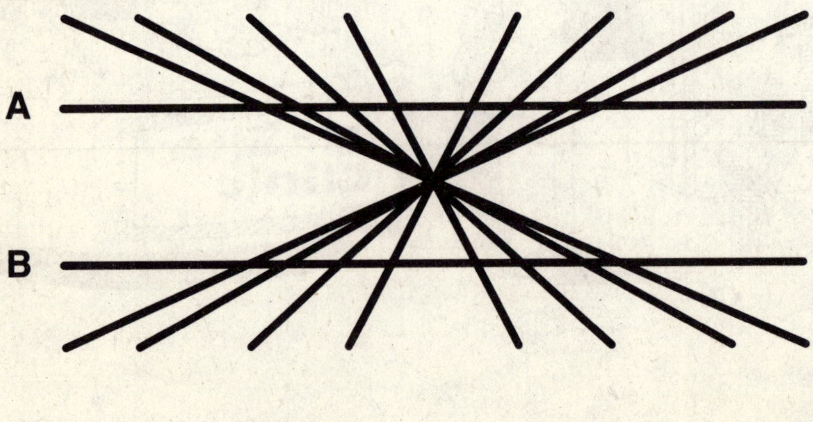

RYAN'S ROCKS

Ryan collects rocks. One day he put 10 pink rocks and 10 white rocks into a cloth bag. He showed the bag to his friend Kyle. Ryan said, "I bet that without looking, I can take out a pair of rocks that are the same color." Kyle blindfolded Ryan to test him. Ryan started to take out the rocks, one by one. What is the smallest number of rocks Ryan has to take out to be sure he has chosen a matching pair?

KYLE'S ROCKS

Kyle put four solid-colored rocks, three striped rocks, and two speckled rocks into a bag. He showed the bag to his friend Ryan. Kyle said, "I bet that without looking, I can take a matching pair of rocks from my bag." Ryan said, "Try it," and blindfolded his friend. Kyle started taking out the rocks, one by one. What is the smallest number of rocks Kyle has to take out to be sure he has chosen a matching pair?

PAPER BUGS

Irma folded a sheet of paper in half and drew half a bug shape along the fold. Irma then cut out the shape to make a bug. Irma kept doing this until she had made six bugs. See if you can match each bug below to the paper it was cut from on the next page.

A

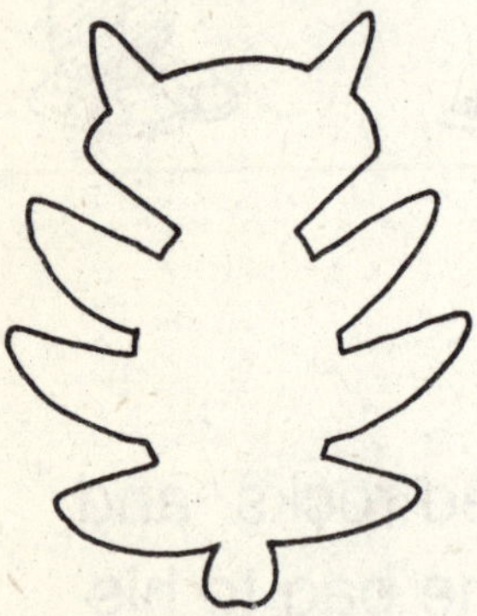

B

C

D

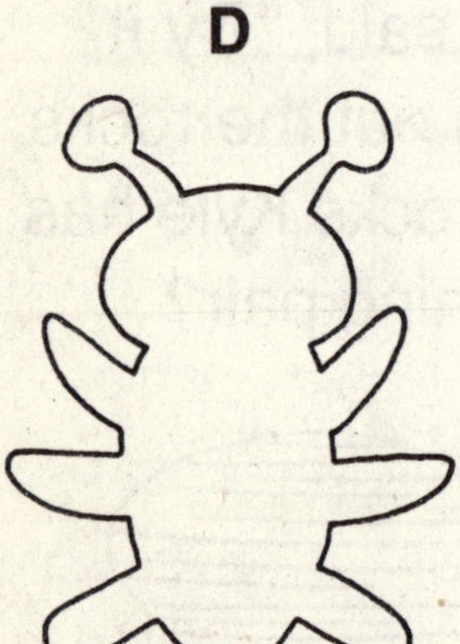

E

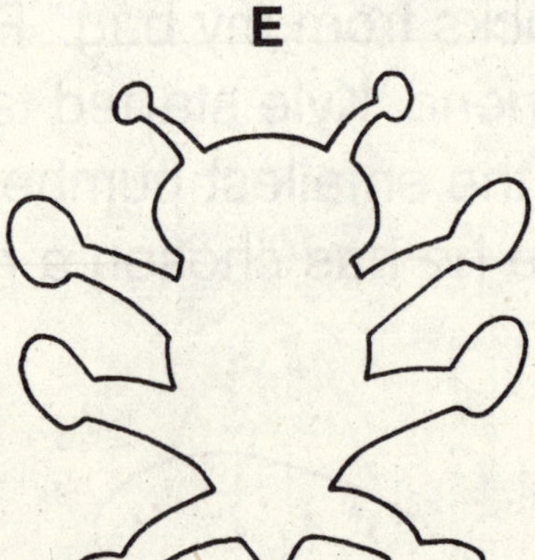

F

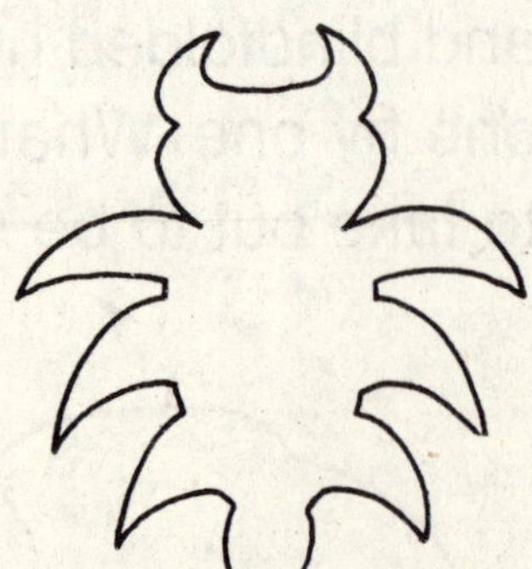

1

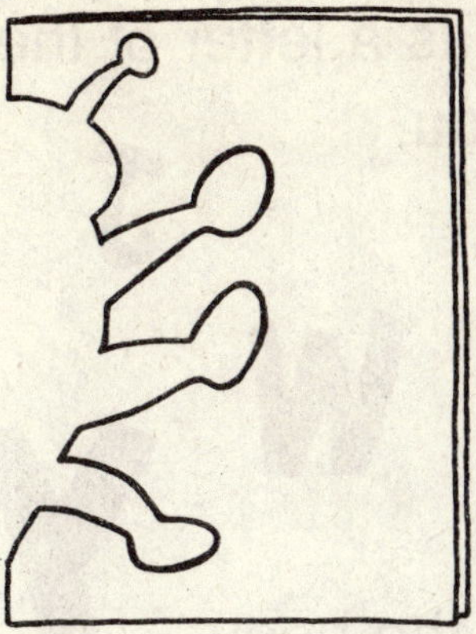

2

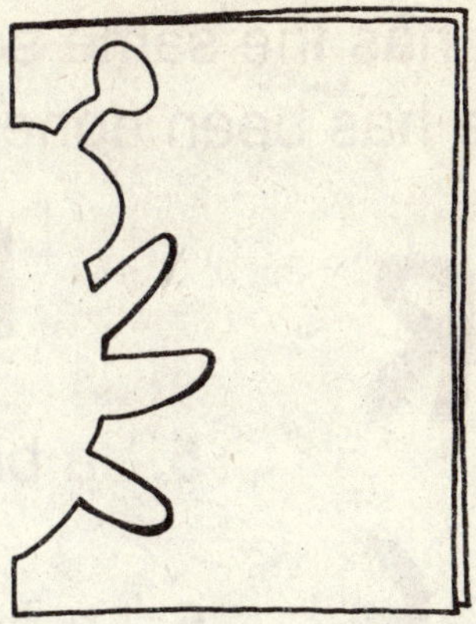

3

4

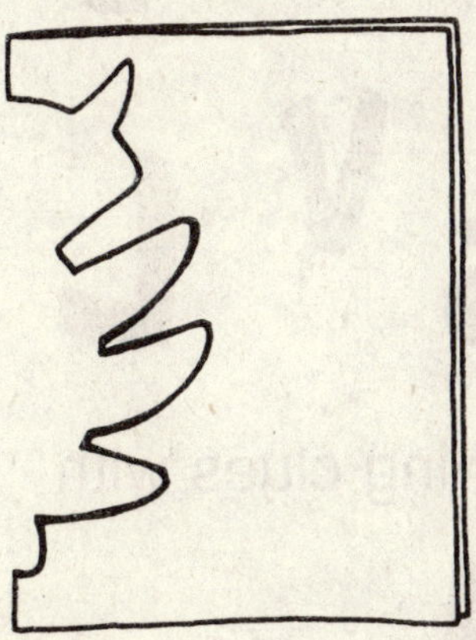

5

6

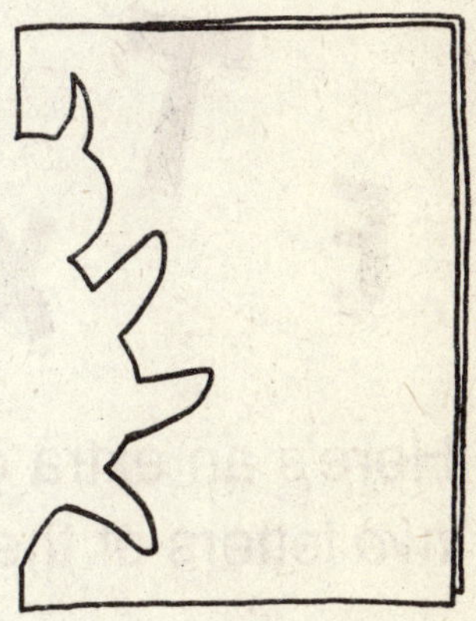

ALPHABET FUN

Try this alphabet challenge! Read the clues below. Each one describes a word that has the same sound as a letter of the alphabet. The first one has been done for you.

1. a hot drink (T)
2. an insect
3. a question word
4. a vegetable
5. a bird
6. a part of the body
7. a large body of water
8. a female sheep

Here's an extra challenge! Answer the following clues with *two* letters of the alphabet.

9. the opposite of full
10. a cone-shaped home

GWEN'S TOWER

Gwen used 26 blocks to build a tower. Can you figure out which tower Gwen built?

A

B

C

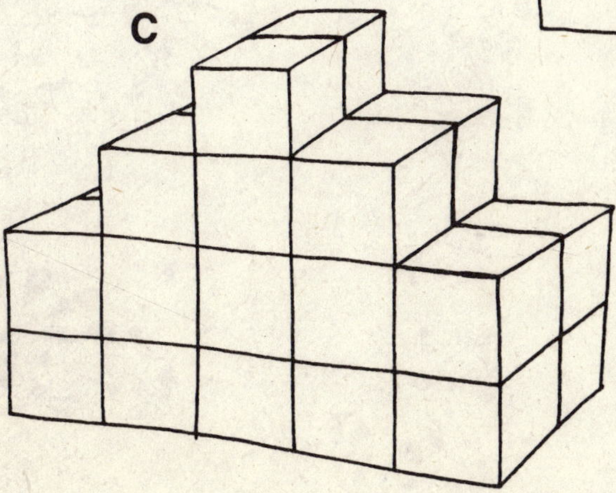

CATS AND DOGS

Get two straws. Place them on the page to divide the cats and dogs into four groups. The groups do not have to have the same number of animals. But within each group, there must be an equal number of cats and dogs.

WORD CONNECTIONS

Look at the groups of words. The words in each group give clues about the missing word. The missing word can be combined with each of the word clues to form compound words. Can you figure out the missing words? The first one has been done for you.

1. foot base room **ball**	**4.** plane line mail ?
2. mark shelf worm ?	**5.** sun flash house ?
3. drop coat bow ?	**6.** bowl gold cat ?

A NEW TOY

Mr. Wood is a toy maker. He makes unusual toys out of wood. One day his helper, Sam, got an idea for a ringtoss game. Sam drew his idea on a sheet of paper. Then he showed the paper to Mr. Wood.

When Mr. Wood looked at the drawing, he shook his head. He said, "Sam, I'd never be able to make that toy."

Look at Sam's idea below. Why can't Mr. Wood make it?

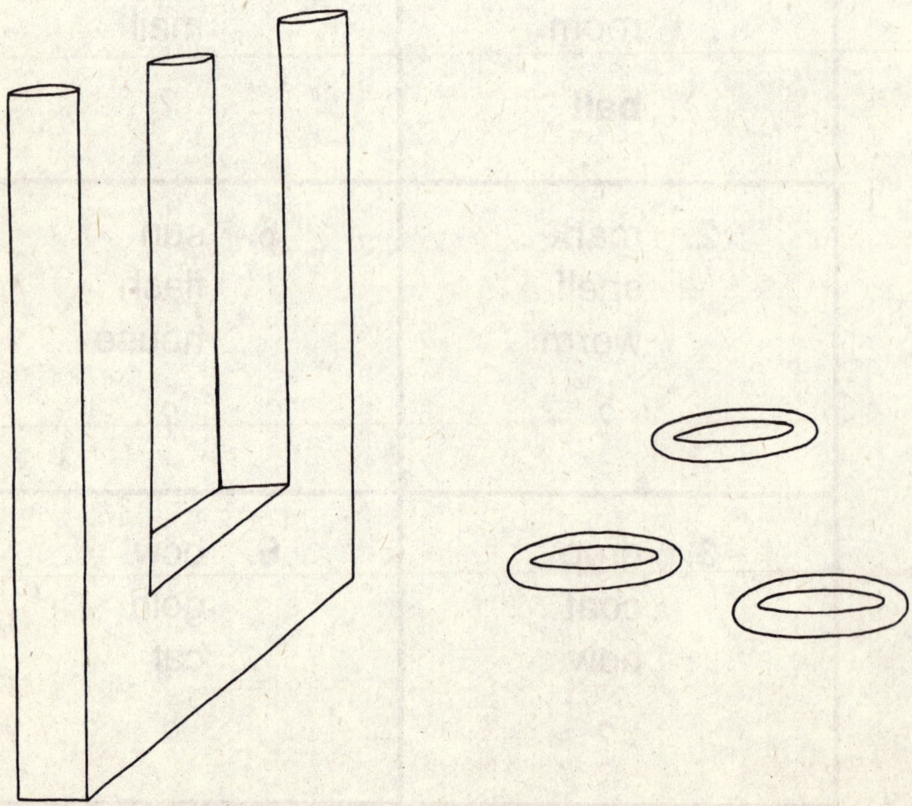

CAN IT BE BUILT?

Mr. Wood is planning to build a wooden toy. He is looking at three interesting designs he might use.

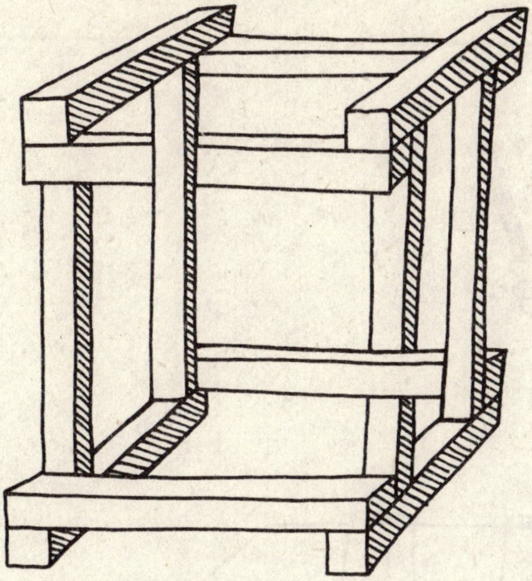

A

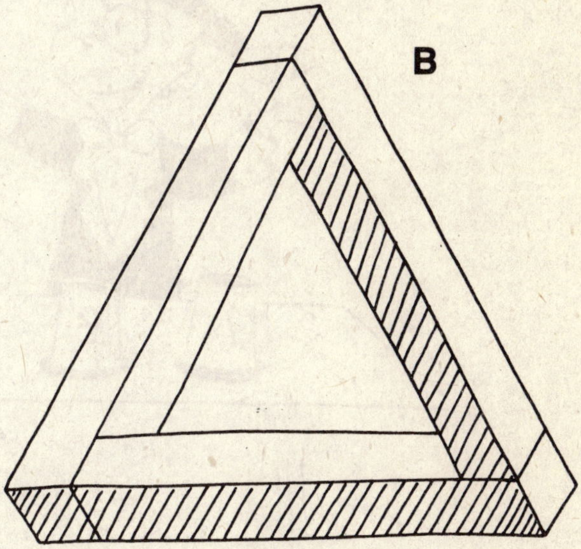

B

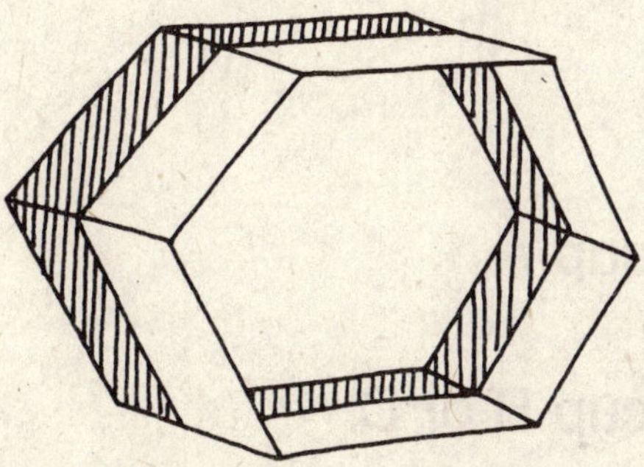

C

Only one of the designs shows an object that can really be built. The other two show things that would be impossible to make. Which design should Mr. Wood use for his toy?

WHERE IS THE BALL?

The magician has hidden a ball under one of the cups on the table. Read the sentences below. Only one of the sentences is true. Where is the ball?

1. The ball is under cup A.

2. The ball is under cup B or D.

3. The ball is under cup A or C.

4. The ball is not under cup B.

ANSWERS

Page 5
A Special Word—NOON
Look in the Mirror—MOM, OTTO

Page 6
From Here to There—The horse's name was Friday.
Horsing Around—The rope was not tied to anything.

Page 7
Move the pennies marked A and B.

Page 8
Two solutions are possible:
planet–plant–plan–pan–an–a
planet–plant–pant–ant–an–a

Page 9
10 lines

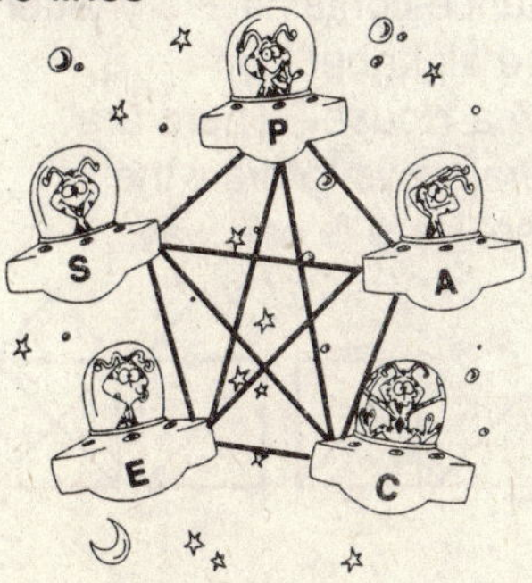

Pages 10 and 11
Each Zop has a matching number of antennae and legs. Each Snarf has a different number of antennae and legs. A and C are Zops; B and D are Snarfs.

Page 12
1. The two sons go across in the boat.
2. One of the sons rows back to Mr. Banks.
3. Mr. Banks rows across the river.
4. The other son rows back to his brother.
5. The two sons go across the river to meet their father.

Page 13
1. Minna takes the cat to Emma's house.
2. She returns to the mouse and the dog.
3. Minna takes the mouse to Emma's house.
4. Minna picks up the cat and returns to the dog.
5. Minna drops off the cat and takes the dog to Emma's house.
6. Minna returns to the cat.
7. Minna takes the cat to Emma's house.

Page 14
Count the Triangles—13 triangles
A Triangle Cat—18 triangles

Page 15
Pieces of Pie

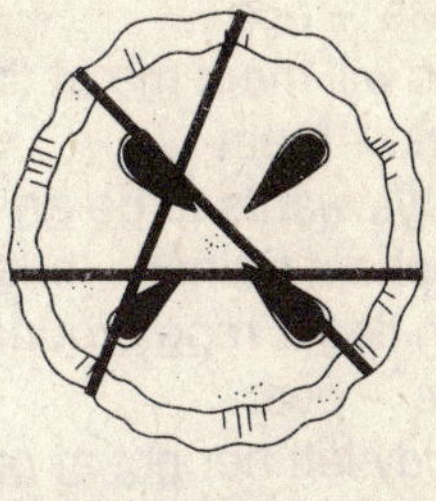

Playing With Food—The spaces between the shapes spell out **HI**.

Page 16
The shadows should be *in front* of the girl and dog because the sun is behind them.

Page 17
Dog on the Run—The lake was frozen.
Parrot Talk—The parrot was deaf.

Page 18
1. Jan will be eleven next week. – bee
2. We planted some corn. – ant
3. The cake batter is thick. – bat
4. Mandy peeled the apple. – eel
5. We will go at six o'clock. – goat
6. Lee got a bar of soap and a towel. – panda
7. Most rich people have big homes. – ostrich
8. Ed will keep the watch or sell it. – horse
9. Dad will need to use a ladder. – seal
10. I think Tom will be a very good student. – beaver

Page 19

1. Bob read a funny story. – bread
2. There are many kinds of beetles. – beet
3. I put four ice cubes in a glass. – rice
4. Kris will meet me at the park. – meat
5. Tanya wants to be an elephant trainer. – bean
6. Len tied a rope around a tree. – pear
7. Cindy left her pot at our house. – potato
8. We need to wrap plenty of string around the box. – apple
9. We hope a chick will hatch from our egg. – peach
10. My sister likes to pick leaves off the ground. – pickle

Page 20

Pennies on a Grid

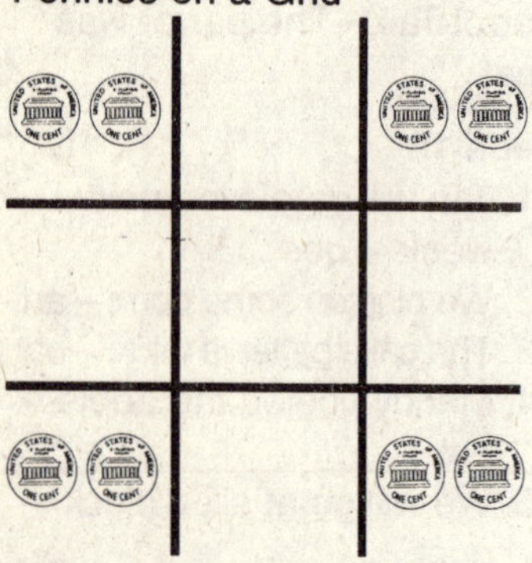

Rows of Pennies

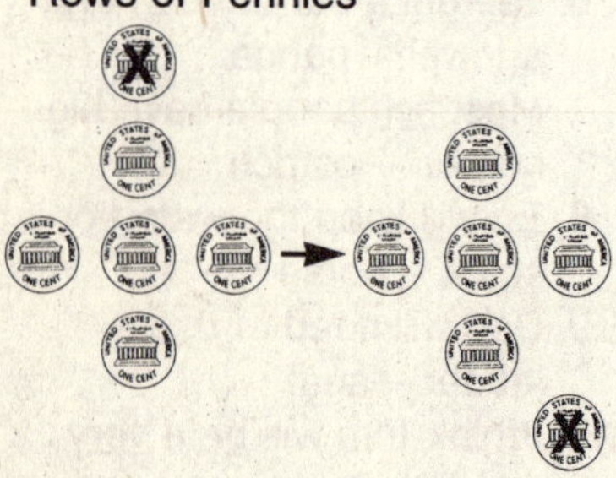

Page 21

A Puzzling Ball Throw—Throw the ball straight up in the air.

Why Can't They Shake Hands?—The children are standing on opposite sides of a door.

Page 22

peas, chicken sandwich, pear, tea, cookie

Page 23

A Cold Drink—An ice cube floats.

On the Road—It was the spare tire in the trunk that was flat.

Page 24

h	a	t
a	p	e
t	e	n

Page 25

s	t	a	r
t	u	n	e
a	n	t	s
r	e	s	t

Page 26

1. B
2. C
3. A
4. C

Page 27

Miss Green is first in line.
Mrs. Brown is second.
Mrs. Black is third.
Miss White is fourth.

Page 28

A puzzle is in the box.

Page 29

There is an **e** in every word, and there is no other vowel in the story.

Page 30

Looking at Lines—All the lines are the same length.

Looking at Circles—The circles are the same size.

Page 31

How Many Blocks?—You may see six blocks with black tops (as though you are looking down on a tower of blocks). Or you may see seven blocks with black bottoms (as though you are looking up at the blocks).

What's in the Piggy Bank?—One quarter, two dimes, and five pennies.

Page 32

The straw should be placed so that the numbers from 10 to 3 are on one side of the straw and the numbers from 4 to 9 are on the other side.

Page 33

A – Jenny
B – Margo
C – Betty
D – Sally
E – Patty

Page 34

The Amazing Waldo—The sentence contains every letter of the alphabet.

Draw a House—There are several ways to draw the house. Here is one way:

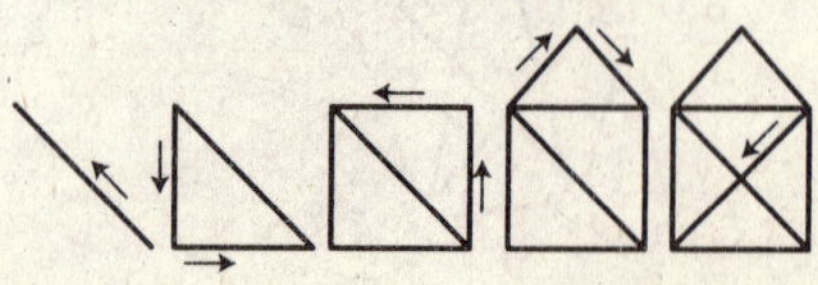

Page 35
Tying a Knot—Cross your arms. (Your left hand will be on top of your right arm and your right hand will be under your left arm, or vice versa.) Then pick up one end of the string with each hand. When you uncross your arms, you will tie a knot.
A Knotty Problem—B forms a knot.

Page 36
Place the bottle on its side. Put your finger in its mouth. Then push the bottle along the table with the paper square still around the neck of the bottle. You are now pushing the bottle through the hole!

Page 37

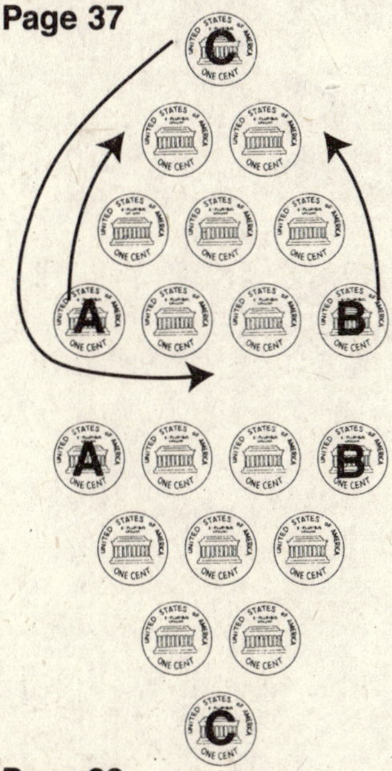

Page 38
The numbers on the clock in the mirror should be reversed.

Page 39
Claudia's bug is a ladybug. It is in the third row, second column.

Pages 40–41
Bo's apartment is on the fourth floor. It is the second one from the left.

Page 42
A Strange Note—Hold the note up to a mirror. It says:

MOM
I AM OUT
WITH MATT.
TOM

Upside-Down Numbers—96

Page 43
Turn the note upside down, then hold it up to a mirror. It says:

MOM
I DECIDED TO
BIKE WITH MIKE.
I WILL COME
HOME SOON.
TOM

Pages 44–45
1. The dog is under the table.
2. We played “Ring Around the Rosie.”
3. You're under arrest.
4. The cat sat on a hat.
5. I was lost in the middle of the forest.
6. Liz bought a pair of pants.
7. Mom drove around in circles.
8. My slippers are under my bed.
9. Jack goes to school far from home.

Page 46
1. No, Pam doesn't like peas. She doesn't like foods that begin with the first letter of her name.
2. Yes, Scott likes cabbage. He likes foods that contain double letters.
3. No, Nicole doesn't like watermelon. She likes foods that have three syllables in their name.

Page 47

1. 
2. 
3. 
4. 
5. 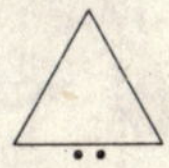

Page 48
There were three Googlies and four Winkles.

Page 49
Mr. Gee owns the dog, Mr. Dee owns the cat, and Mrs. Jay owns the rabbit.

Page 50
Which Lines Meet?—Line A would meet Line C.
Which Line Is Straight?—Both lines are straight.

Page 51
Ryan's Rocks—Ryan needs to take out three rocks.
Kyle's Rocks—Kyle needs to take out four rocks.

Pages 52–53
A – 4
B – 6
C – 5
D – 2
E – 1
F – 3

Page 54

1. T
2. B
3. Y
4. P
5. J
6. I
7. C
8. U
9. MT
10. TP

Page 55

Gwen built B.

Page 56

Page 57

1. ball
2. book
3. rain
4. air
5. light
6. fish

Page 58

Though the object looks like one solid piece, it really isn't. If you follow the lines with your finger, you'll find that the three "poles" are not connected.

Page 59

Mr. Wood should use design C.

Page 60

Sentence 2 is true. The ball is under cup B.